Aberdeenshire Library and Information Service
www.aberdeenshire.gov.uk.libraries
Renewals Hotline 01224 661511

7.9.09

VAUGHAN, Jenny

Does it flow?

Does it flow?
All about liquids

Jenny Vaughan
Experiments by Meredith Blakeney

W
FRANKLIN WATTS
LONDON•SYDNEY

First published in 2009
by Franklin Watts

Copyright © Franklin Watts 2009

Franklin Watts
338 Euston Road
London NW1 3BH

Franklin Watts Australia
Level 17/207 Kent Street
Sydney, NSW 2000

Series editor: Sarah Peutrill
Art director: Jonathan Hair
Design: Elaine Wilkinson
Photographs: Paul Bricknell (unless otherwise credited)

With thanks to our models: Conah Caple, Mary Conquest, Lily Cornelius, Katie Lloyd, Chris Penny, Darnell Smith.

Picture credits: Alamy: 21t (MEB-Photography); John Alston: 14b; Corbis: 9t (Dex Image); I Stock Photo: 8t (Saltov), 23t (Jeremkin), 29 (Danakia); NASA: 16r; Shutterstock: 1, 5b (Peter Zurek), 1, 9b (Monkey Business Images), 4l (Vadim Kolobanov), 4r (Christina Richards), 5t (Jaimie Duplass), 8b (Lukáš Hejtman), 10t (Tyler Olson), 10b (Khomulo Anna), 11 (Andy Z), 14t (Stephen Finn), 15t (Diane N. Ennis), 17t (Petrov Andrey), 17b (Sebastien Burel), 20t (kojoku), 20b (Svetlana Privezentseva), 21bl (Ekaterina Shlikhunova), 21br (Ilkka Kukko), 22t (Les Scholz), 22b (Tania Zbrodko), 23b (Palto), 26t (Sybille Yates), 26b (John Wollwerth), 27t (Izaokas Sapiro), 28t (Patricia Hofmeester), 28b (Mates); Wishlist Images: 6, 7, 27b.
Cover images: Shutterstock: tl (Jaimie Duplass), tm (Sebastien Burel), tr (Svetlana Privezentseva), b (Peter Zurek)

Dewey number: 530.4

ISBN 978 0 7496 8721 2

Printed in China

Franklin Watts is a division of Hachette Children's Books, an Hachette UK company.

www.hachette.co.uk

Contents

The topics highlighted above are investigations you can try.

Words in **bold** are in the glossary on page 30.

What is a liquid?

A liquid is any **material** that behaves like water. Except when it is a tiny drop, a liquid has no shape of its own. Instead, it takes the shape of any container it is in – although it may not fill it.

'States of matter'

Materials can be in three main forms. These are solids, liquids and gases. For example, water can be in the form of solid ice, or a liquid, or a gas, called **water vapour**. Solids have a definite shape, which does not easily change. Gases have no shape, and they can spread out to fill the container they are in. They are nearly always invisible, though we may sometimes be able to smell them.

The water in this vat of apple juice becomes a gas called water vapour when it is hot.

Water in a solid form is ice.

Flowing

Liquids **flow**, which means they pour along pipes or **channels** or just along the ground. Left to themselves, liquids will flow downwards. This is because the **force** we call **gravity** pulls them downwards.

The force of gravity makes liquids flow downwards. This ketchup is flowing down from the bottle.

Some liquids are runny. If you pour them onto a floor, they spread out quickly into a puddle. Runny liquids flow down a slope quickly. Other liquids are thick, and do not spread out or flow very fast. When a liquid is very thick, and flows slowly, we say it is **viscous**. Examples of viscous liquids are syrup, ketchup and thick engine oil.

The thick **lava** that comes out of some **volcanoes** can be extremely viscous. It flows very slowly down mountainsides.

Floating and sinking

You will need:

A small bowl, a jug full of water, a tray, a ping-pong ball, a pebble about the same size as the ball, plus a few more pebbles, a nail, a cork, a small toy, cooking oil.

Try this experiment to find out about **floating**.

Fill the bowl with water and place it carefully on the tray. Place the ping-pong ball gently in the water. What happens?

Repeat the experiment using the pebble. What happens?

The ping-pong ball and the pebble have the same volume (they are the same size). The ping-pong ball is lighter than the same volume of water. We say it is less **dense** than water, and it **floats**. The pebble is heavier than the same volume of water. It is more dense, and sinks.

Now try pushing the ping-pong ball down to the bottom of the bowl.

3

Can you feel the water pushing it upwards towards the surface? This pushing is called **upthrust**. It stops the ball from sinking. There is upthrust when you place the pebble in the bowl, too. But the pebble is heavy, and the upthrust is not strong enough to stop it from sinking.

Select some other objects and see if they will float – for example, a nail, a cork and a small toy.

4

Can liquids float on other liquids? Try pouring cooking oil on the water and see.

What happens?

Put lots of pebbles in the bowl. Keep adding pebbles. Look at the level of the water in the bowl. What happens to it?

A liquid's skin

A liquid has a very thin, stretchy skin over it. The skin forms from the tiny particles called **molecules** that make up the liquid. These pull towards each other and, when they are on the surface of the liquid, they pull especially hard. They are what holds a drop of liquid in its round shape. We call the skin **surface tension**.

Surface tension holds a drop of water in a round shape.

Walking on a pond

The surface tension of water is weak – but it is strong enough for very light objects to sit on it. This makes it possible for a paperclip or a needle to sit on the surface of the water, even though metal is denser than water. It can stay on the surface until you stir up the water and break the skin. Surface tension makes it possible for some kinds of insects to run across the water.

This insect is called a pond-skater – because it can 'skate' or run across the surface tension that covers the pond's surface.

A traditional way of shaping glass is to blow air into molten glass. The glass is stretchy while it is hot, with a thin skin, and can be shaped. As is cools, it becomes solid.

Bubbles

A round shape is the easiest shape for surface tension to hold – which is why raindrops and **bubbles** are round. Bubbles are like small balloons, surrounded by a skin of surface tension. This skin is not stretchy enough to hold the air inside the bubbles for long. But soap or detergent makes the skin much more stretchy, and bubbles last longer.

You can buy special liquid for blowing bubbles. You blow through a wire or plastic circle.

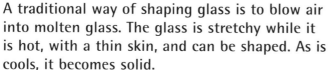

Liquid force

Moving liquids have force, which means they can move things. We can see this if we place an object in moving water. The water may carry it along, or, if it cannot do that, it will push it out of its way.

Water wheels are one of the oldest ways in which the force of flowing water has been used to power machinery.

Rivers

Rivers flow downhill, pulled by the force of gravity. Flowing water pushes its way though soil and soft rock, carrying some along with it. In this way, the river water makes a channel for itself. The force is greater if there is a lot of water flowing fast. In the past, it was common to use the force of flowing water to turn wheels that worked the machinery in flour **mills** (above). A few mills like these still exist.

As a stream tumbles down a mountain, it moves fast. It carves out a channel for itself among the rocks and soil.

Hydroelectricity

Today, one of the most important ways the force of moving water is used is to make electricity. Often, a dam is built across the river, and a lake called a reservoir, containing a huge amount of water, builds up behind it. The water pushes through gaps in the dam with great force. This turns wheels, called turbines, which work machines that make electricity. Electricity made in this way is called **hydroelectricity**, or hydropower.

The water in a reservoir presses against the dam wall with great force. As the water passes through holes in the dam, it turns wheels called turbines, which are used to make electricity.

Make a water wheel

A water wheel or turbine is a wheel with blades. The moving water catches each blade in turn, and the force makes the wheel go round. You can make your own water wheel.

You will need:
A plastic-coated paper plate, scissors, a pencil, a tap.

Make six L-shaped cuts around 2cm deep, at equal distances around the outside edge of the plate.

Bend these to make the blades around the edge of the wheel.

Push the pencil through the middle of the plate and move it backwards and forwards several times so that the plate spins easily. You may need to ask an adult to help with this. For example, you may need to use a nail or another sharp object to make the hole, and you should not do this by yourself.

3

Now turn on the tap and hold your pencil so that the water catches one of the blades of the water wheel. What happens?

4

Your water wheel may move quite gently, but the great power of water flowing through a dam can turn the huge turbines much faster, and create electricity for thousands of homes.

Now experiment

Can you think of other ways to make blades for your wheel? Experiment with different designs and see which works the best.

Lifting and pushing

The force of liquids is useful in other ways as well. One way they help us is in machines that lift or move heavy objects. These machines use a **hydraulic** system.

This digger uses a hydraulic system to lift very heavy loads.

How it works

In a hydraulic system, there is a container filled with liquid, with two pipes leading from it, one wide and one narrow. These, too, have liquid in them. If liquid is pushed down the wide pipe, it goes into the container. But there is no room for any extra liquid there. To make space for it, the amount of liquid that was pushed downwards travels up another pipe. The force of the liquid moving upwards is enough to move objects.

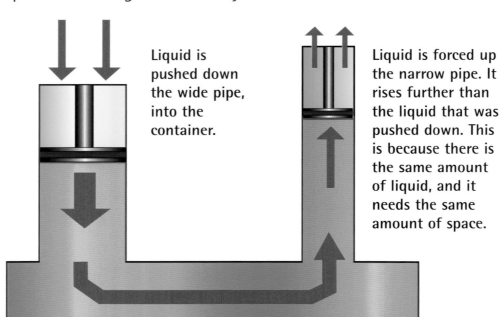

Liquid is pushed down the wide pipe, into the container.

Liquid is forced up the narrow pipe. It rises further than the liquid that was pushed down. This is because there is the same amount of liquid, and it needs the same amount of space.

Using hydraulic systems

Hydraulic systems are used in many machines such as lifts, cranes and diggers. They are also used to make the brakes on a car work. The liquid used in these systems is usually oil.

The boom (arm) of this crane is raised and lowered using a hydraulic system.

You can push water. Fill a plastic bottle with water. Ask an adult to help you fix a sausage-shaped balloon over the end of the bottle. Squeeze the bottle – and watch how water fills the balloon.

Water for life

Water is the most common liquid on Earth, and it is the most important. Nothing on our planet can live without it. That is why, when scientists want to know if there can be life on other planets, they look first for water. If there is water, there may be life.

Plants

Plants draw up water through their roots. It travels through their stems into their leaves, flowers and fruits. Some plants need a lot of water. Others can survive in dry desert areas, with very little water. But even these must take in some water – or they will die.

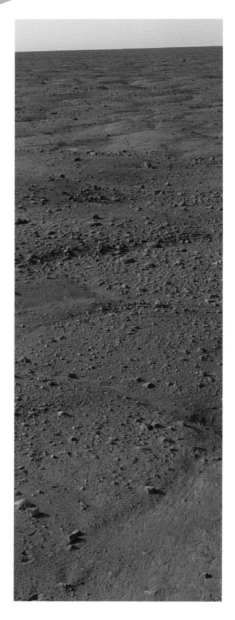

See how plants can store water in their fruits. With an adult to help, cut an orange in half and squeeze out the juice. This juice is almost all water.

Scientists believe there may be water on the planet Mars. If there is, there is a chance that there may be living things there too – but probably only very small, simple life forms.

The jerboa is like a small rat, and lives in the deserts of Africa and Asia. It gets all the water it needs from the beetles and seeds it eats.

Animals and water

Different animals, too, need different amounts of water. Adult humans need around two litres every day. We take this in when we drink, and from our food. It keeps our bodies working properly. We can live for several weeks without eating – but only a few days without drinking. Some animals need very little water. There are desert animals, for example, that get all they need from the food they eat.

The African grasslands, where these zebras live, are very dry. The zebras must come to a river or water hole to drink. Without water, they will die.

How plants take up water

The stems of plants contain tiny tubes, and water rises up these. This process is called **capillary** action. It happens because of the way water molecules pull towards each other. In a narrow tube, the molecules pull each other upwards. Capillary action is how plants draw up water from the soil up their stems.

Ask an adult to cut 1cm off the bottom (wide end) of both sticks of celery. Half-fill two glasses with water.

1

Put one stick of celery into one glass of water with the wide end at the bottom. Add a bottle of red food dye to the other glass and put the other stick of celery into it.

2

3

Next day, have a look at your two sticks of celery. Hold the celery up to the light. What do you notice?

You will see a streak of red colour inside celery standing in coloured water, but not the other. You will also see red dots at the top of the celery stick. This shows how the coloured water has risen through the stem.

Get experimenting

Try the experiment with other plants. How could you make a white flower blue?

Liquids to solids – and back again

Water becomes solid ice when it is cooled to 0° Celsius. Other liquids become solids at different temperatures.

When the weather is very cold, solid ice may form on lakes or ponds.

Melting

Some materials are solid at normal temperatures, but become liquids when they are heated. We say they **melt**. Materials that melt include ice, metals, the tar on roads, plastics, glass and even rocks. Many of our foods, such as butter, ice cream and chocolate, also melt. The temperature at which a solid melts is called its melting point. Many metals, for example, must be very hot indeed to melt, so we say they have a high melting point. Butter has a low melting point.

As the ice melts from this **glacier**, streams of water flow down the mountain.

Solidifying

Materials that melt will only remain liquid while they are at a temperature above their melting point. As they cool, they solidify – become solid again. We can use melting and solidifying as a way to shape the materials. For example, a chocolate-maker may pour melted chocolate into a **mould**. As it cools, the chocolate takes the shape of the mould, and then hardens into that shape. This method is used in industry to shape materials such a glass, plastic and metals.

This man is spreading hot **asphalt**, or tar, on the road. It will become hard when it cools, but can melt again in very hot weather.

Melted chocolate has been poured into this mould. As it cooled, it hardened and became a rabbit shape.

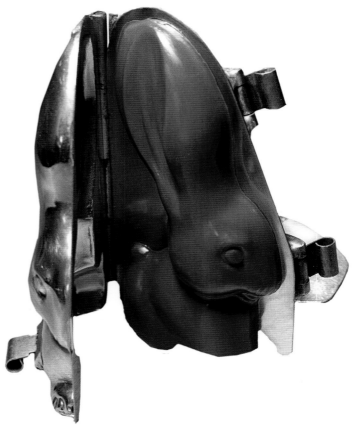

Liquids into gas

Liquids can change to gases, for example, if they are warmed. Gases can become liquids if they are cooled or put under pressure.

Warm sunshine soon turns the water in wet washing to vapour and dries the clothes.

Water vapour

When water changes to the gas water vapour, we say it has **evaporated**. Evaporation dries out wet washing, and damp soil. It draws water out of the leaves of plants, and from ponds, rivers lakes and the sea. We cannot see, feel or smell water vapour, but it is all around us in the air. It will turn back into liquid water if it is cooled.

If you look at a cold surface, like the outside of a cold drinks can on a hot day, you will see that water drops have formed on the outside. Water vapour in the air has **condensed** on the side of the can.

The water cycle

Water vapour plays an important part in our weather. Air containing water vapour rises high above the Earth's surface. It cools, and the vapour condenses and falls back to Earth as rain. We call this whole process the **water cycle**.

1. As the Sun shines over the Earth, water evaporates and becomes water vapour.

2. The water rises high in the sky, and cools to form clouds. We say it has condensed into tiny droplets of water.

3. The droplets join together and become heavier. These fall back to Earth as rain.

Rain will soon fall from these clouds.

How the water cycle works

You can see how the water cycle works by doing this experiment.

Put the water in the bowl.

1

Put the small cup in the middle of the bowl and cover the bowl with cling film. Place a small stone in the centre of the cling film, directly over the small cup, to weigh the cling film down.

2

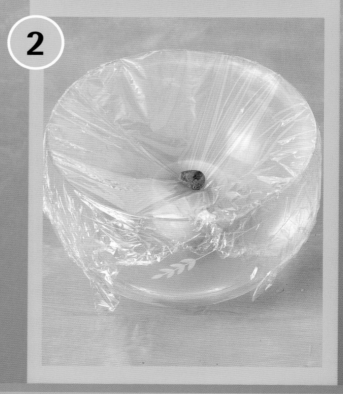

Place the bowl in a warm place for several hours then look in the small cup. Beads of water form on the cling film, and drip into the cup. The water in the large bowl evaporated (turned into gas). It then re-formed (condensed) on the underside of the cling film, and dripped into the cup.

Repeat the experiment. This time, mix three teaspoonfuls of salt with the water in the bowl. It will taste salty. When the experiment is finished, taste the water in the cup. What do you notice?

3

4

Get experimenting

Try the experiment again.
This time, mix different things in the warm water. Try food colouring, or instant coffee. Is the water that condenses coloured?

Liquids in industry

As well as being used to make hydroelectricity (see page 12), water is used in other kinds of power stations and in factories, to keep machinery cool. It is important in papermaking, in making and using dyes and inks, and much more. However, there is another important liquid used in **industry**. It is oil.

This is a paper mill. Paper is made using lots of water.

What is oil?

When we talk about oil in industry, we usually mean oil that is pumped from under the ground. It formed millions of years ago, from dead plants and sea animals. Their bodies sank to the ocean floor and, gradually, were covered by rocks. There, they changed to become oil. Oil is found in many places on Earth – often where there is no longer any sea.

These huge tanks have oil stored in them.

Oils **lubricate** machinery, so that it runs smoothly.

Using oil

Oil is the most important **fuel** there is. The engines of vehicles such as cars, trains and aircraft burn oil. It is used as fuel in many factories. Oil also helps to make machinery run smoothly. A thin layer of oil helps the moving parts slip over each other easily, and not get stuck. We say it lubricates them.

Try picking up a square of jelly with chopsticks. See what happens if you cover the jelly with vegetable oil. Why is it more difficult?

Liquids at home

As in industry, the two most important liquids we use at home are water and oil. As well as using water for drinking and washing, it is also used in cooking, to water plants, to fill the radiators in our heating systems and in many other ways. Fuel oil is used to heat many homes, and to run our cars. We also use oil for lubricating locks, cars and bicycles.

We use vegetable oil in cooking.

Other liquids

Most liquids we use at home contain oil or water. Paint usually has one or both liquids in it. Soft drinks and milk both contain water, and so do many of our foods. We use special oils made from plants for cooking and to make margarine.

Vegetable oils are made from sunflower or other seeds, or olives. They help make food tastier, and stop it sticking to pans.

Special floor cleaners
make it easier for water to
lift the dirt from the surface.

Cleaning fluids

There are special liquids that help water get
rid of dirt. These are detergents, or cleaning
fluids. They change oils to make it easier
for water to wash them away. They help
dissolve other kinds of dirt, too, and make
them easier to wipe away.

Try washing up
greasy plates with just
water. What do you notice?
Now try using washing-up
liquid. You can see how the
washing-up liquid breaks up
the film of oil, and makes
it possible to wash
it away.

Glossary

asphalt A sticky, black liquid made from coal, and used to make roads.

blade A flat, wide part of something.

bubble A ball of gas surrounded by a film of liquid.

capillary A very tiny tube. Capillary action is the way liquids automatically rise up very tiny tubes.

channel A dip in the ground that has been cut or worn away.

condense To change from being a gas to a liquid – when a gas is cooled, it will usually condense to form a liquid.

dense When molecules are tightly packed within a material.

evaporate To change from being a liquid into a gas – for example, when it is warmed, water changes from liquid water into a gas called water vapour.

float To be held up by a liquid or gas. For example, a balloon will float on water, and will also float in the air.

flow To move or run like a stream.

force A push or a pull – something that moves an object, or stops it or changes its direction.

fuel Something that is burned to make heat or power.

glacier A river of ice that slides slowly down a mountainside.

gravity A natural force that draws objects towards the centre of the Earth.

hydraulic Operated by moving liquids.

hydroelectricity Electricity made using the force of moving water. This is usually water from a dam, which is forced over turbines (large wheels) to make them turn.

industry Factories that make things.

lava Hot, melted rock that flows out of some volcanoes when they erupt.

lubricate To make smooth and slippery using oil or grease.

material A material can be in three main forms – solid, liquid or gas.

melt To change something from a solid to a liquid by warming it.

mill A machine for grinding up grain.

molecule The smallest particle of a substance.

mould A hollow shape which melted materials can be put into. When they harden, they take the shape of the mould.

pressure Pushing on a material – when something is under pressure it is being pushed from all directions.

surface tension A film that forms over the surface of a liquid.

upthrust An upward push.

viscous A thick, heavy liquid, like syrup.

volcano A hole in the Earth's crust. Sometimes, a mountain forms around it. Melted rock and ash from under the Earth is forced to the surface through the volcano.

water cycle The way that water evaporates from the surface of the Earth, rises into the sky as water vapour and then falls back to Earth as liquid water.

water vapour Water in the form of a gas.

Some answers

Page 7: Yes, cooking oil will definitely float on water. Even if you mix it into the water, it will rise to the top after a while. As you add pebbles, the water level will rise. This is because the pebbles are more dense than water. They sink and push the water out of the way.

Page 13: Another way to make a blade for a water wheel would be to cut slits in the edge of the paper plate and slide in rectangles of card, so they are at right-angles to the plate. You could also try making a wheel from two plates, with blades between them, which is more like a real-life water wheel.

Page 15: This experiment shows that you can push water from one space into another. It does not show how the same amount of water pushes further along a narrow pipe than along a wide one. Can you devise an experiment to show how this happens?

Page 19: It depends on the flower and the colouring you use, but you can usually get a white carnation, for example, to turn blue by placing its stem in a vase of blue-coloured water.

Page 25: If you try the experiment using salty water, the water in the cup won't be salty, because the salt won't evaporate. It will remain behind with the water that is left in the bowl. If you put colouring of any kind in the water, this too will be left behind when the water evaporates.

Pages 27: The oil will make the jelly very slippery, because it will have lubricated it. It will be very hard to pick it up with the chopsticks.

Index

Further information

www.bbc.co.uk/schools/ks2bitesize/science/revision_bites/gases2.shtml
Basic facts about liquids.

www.bbc.co.uk/schools/digger/5_7entry/8continue.shtml
For younger users – about floating and sinking.

www.bbc.co.uk/schools/ks2bitesize/science/revision_bites/changing_state2.shtml
The water cycle.

www.reuk.co.uk/Introduction-to-Water-Wheels.htm
Water wheels in real life.

www.epa.gov/nps/kids/TENSION.HTM
More about surface tension.

http://science.howstuffworks.com/hydraulic1.htm
Basic facts about how hydraulics work – a bit difficult, but with good pictures.

www.manatee.k12.fl.us/sites/elementary/samoset/1water.htm
A site about water, and why we need it.

http://dwb.unl.edu/teacher/nsf/c01/c01links/ga.water.usgs.gov/edu/capillaryaction.html
How capillary action works.

www.bbc.co.uk/schools/ks2bitesize/science/revision_bites/changing_state1.shtml
States of matter – how materials are solids, liquids or gases and can often change from one to another.